A Brief Look at Earth's Beautiful, Chaotic Climate

Published by D. L. Bjorngjeld
Forest Lake, Minnesota

ISBN 978-0-9981110-3-2

Layout & Design by Todd Anderson

Printed in United States of America

A Brief Look at Earth's Beautiful, Chaotic Climate

Acknowledgement

I'd like to offer my "mea culpa" right from the get-go. Fourteen years ago, when I started making notes on the subject of Global Warming, I failed to write down whose comments or whose ideas I was scribbling on the page. At that time I had no idea I would eventually put them together in a book, and felt no need to know the person's name for future acknowledgement.

This book is now a compilation of all those notes and ideas, so I plead guilty for plagiarizing ideas and quotes and, in most cases, couldn't even tell you which specific ideas are taken from whom. As an accumulation they form my thoughts on the subject.

In this case, I hope those whose ideas I've taken are forgiving; since this book is not for personal profit (I'd be surprised if I even recover cost... Poor me) rather, this is another voice against the preposterous notion of Man-Made Global Warming and the dangerous "remedies" proposed. (The cure is far worse then the alleged ailment.)

Preface

Our Beautiful, Warm, Comfortable World

I feel very fortunate to be living at a time when Earth's climate is warm and comfortable. It has been slowly warming since the Little Ice Age, a glacial period that's only 170 years in our past. The places affected most by glaciers back then were Europe, North Atlantic area, Alaska, New Zealand, the Andes, and other parts of South America.

During that time, extremely cold, long winters, along with the short, cool, wet summers caused crop failure, famine, and population decline (death) throughout much of Europe. Most of Greenland collapsed because of starvation.

The warming we've been experiencing in recent decades has helped extend our growing seasons, improved crop yields, and allowed for better living conditions for us humans. Life expectancy when we exited the Little Ice Age was about 40 years. Today it's 75 worldwide, and 79 years in the United States.

Meanwhile, for two decades, we've been *lectured to* and *brow-beaten* that we're on the verge of destroying our planet by emitting CO_2.

CO2 is not a pollutant! Carbon is the basis of all life, and CO2 is where plants and trees get it. Below a level of 150 ppm (parts per million) photosynthesis ceases and plant life dies. All life would likely be gone in two years if that occurred. We've been too close (as low as 180 ppm) a couple of times in our history. Photosynthesis is one of the first things that we learn about in science class. (Remember?)

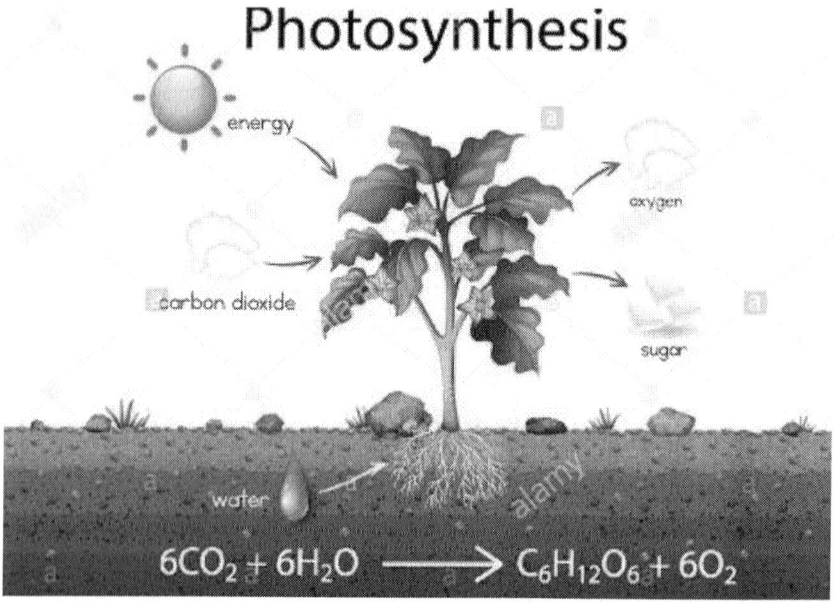

We humans have improved Earth's health in the last hundred years, by helping increase the CO2 level from 280 ppm up to today's 405 ppm. This increase of CO2 has caused the "greening" of our planet, with more and more vegetation showing in satellite photos. At the level of 405 ppm, many scientists contend we are still, "*a CO2 starved planet*."

The 2006 predictions of Al Gore in, "An Inconvenient Truth," included his opinion that because of our CO_2 emissions, the planet would warm uncontrollably, and sea levels would rise 20 feet in the next decade. As a result, many of our coastal States would be partially flooded, while much of Florida would be lost to the Atlantic Ocean. **Now, 13 years later... *What's happened?*** (And *why* did Al "Oscar" Gore purchase a $9 Million beachfront mansion in Montecito, California?)

Gore also contends that CO_2 is what controls global warming... More than the sun... More than water in all its forms (gas, liquid, and solid)... More than the oceans.... So, something around **0.00**16% of our atmosphere *is the increase of CO_2 caused by human emissions.* That's about one molecule of CO_2 in every 85,000 molecules of the atmosphere that is causing the warming according to the Prophet Gore and His Disciples *(now that it's Orthodoxy).*

Back in 2005, when I first took interest in this subject and began researching on Wikipedia and Google, as well as reading a number of books on it, Al Gore's theories just didn't seem to add up.

One of the more unfortunate by-products of my "research," was learning something about the nature and evolution of truthfulness and ethics in anything remotely involving politics. Fortunately, as I did my research on Google and Wikipedia, I printed out everything that seemed important.

Now, 14 years later, much of it is *not available* on Google or Wikipedia, and much of what *is available* has been edited or rewritten. And, interestingly, it's always slanted to the benefit of the Warmist Ideology (Theology).

Every day, temperatures rise and fall through day and night. A day is simply a 24-hour cycle and temperatures vary through the course of each day.

Every year, temperatures rise and fall through spring, summer, fall, and winter. A year is simply a 365-day cycle and temperatures vary through the seasons.

These two cycles happen automatically. We can neither change them nor stop them, any more than we can stop the Earth's rotation.

(Please bear with me as I attempt to describe Earth's complex climate in a few paragraphs.)

Earth's Climate System is primarily the confluence of two turbulent fluid systems (the oceans and the atmosphere) constantly interacting with each other. *Turbulent* meaning they are characterized by irregular circulations. *Interacting* meaning the oceans and the atmosphere exchange heat with each other, and exert a stress on each other. Added to that stress is the fact that these fluid systems are situated on a planet that is rotating on its axis and revolving around the sun. This causes them to be unevenly heated by the sun. Uneven heating is what causes the movement of these "fluid" systems. The tropics would be much warmer and the poles would be much colder if it were not for this movement.

Oceans have circulations and currents operating on time scales ranging from years to millennia. The circulations and currents bring heat and CO_2 to and from the ocean's surface.

The atmosphere interacts with the oceans *and* with the Earth's hugely irregular land surface. The mountain ranges of the Himalayas, the Rockies, the Andes and many others are continuously forcing air to flow over and around them. These irregular air flows greatly disturb the atmosphere.

Water (in solid, liquid, and vapor phases) is a vital constituent in our climate system. Heat is required to change ice to liquid, and liquid to water vapor. And, obviously, the reverse is also truc. The release of energy when water vapor condenses will drive cumulonimbus clouds to towering heights. The energy produced by this process is *immense*. Water vapor and high cirrus clouds are far and away the largest component of the "greenhouse gases."

Added to all of this are the many influences of the Milankovitch Cycles, the South Pacific Convergence, soil-moisture, permafrost, Southern Oscillations, North Atlantic Oscillations, El Niño, Intertropical Convergence, the Hadley Circulation, the Madden-Julian Oscillation, atmospheric blocking, tropical cyclones, storm tracks, jet streams and more.

So, our Climate is Extremely Complex!

Meanwhile, for two decades, the proponents of "Man-Made Global Warming" insist on roughly the following as their narrative on how they can control this complex system: *"The influence on climate, an extremely complex, multi-factored system, can be described and summarized in <u>one variable</u> -* ***globally averaged temperature change can be controlled by controlling the single variable of carbon dioxide (CO2) caused by human emissions."***

They simply ignore the *immense systems* influencing climate and say, ***"It's the CO2, stupid."*** Even though the amount of CO2 emissions caused by human activity (3%) is dwarfed by natural causes (97% - oceans, volcanoes, trees, plants, and more).

I'm flabbergasted that any reasonable person could accept this "logic."

* * * *

If you're anything like me, your eyes glaze over when trying to read long, complicated explanations, involving "in-the-weeds" details. So, I've attempted to condense the pertinent information on each subject into short chapters.

I only hope you read it through and then do your own research to reach a conclusion.

A Brief Look at Earth's Ice Ages

"TIME is a 4-letter word" (I stole that from Ian Plimer, Australian Geologist and Professor). And it is the arch-enemy of Man-Made Global Warming. We've been waiting nearly three decades for any sign of "*Catastrophic Warming*" as predicted.

Studying TIME can help in understanding Earth's climate and climate changes. Ever since the Earth was formed (it was on a Tuesday, 4½ billion years ago) there has been continual climate change.

In terms of Earth's climate, we are not currently living in extraordinary times (unfortunately for the disciples of man-made global warming). Looking at the big picture, we are living in rather ordinary, boring, yet comfortable times. For about 80% of TIME, Earth has been ***warmer and wetter than today... And ice free***. During 20% of TIME, *Earth's climate has been as cold as now, and had ice.*

There have been five major ice ages in Earth's TIME (most of them occurred before we humans appeared on the planet):

1. Huronian Ice Age
2. Cryogenian Ice Age
3. Andean-Saharan Ice Age
4. Karoo or Paleozoic Ice Age
5. Quaternary Ice Age

The first major Ice Age occurred about 2½ billion years ago. It covered a good portion of the Earth's surface with ice. How did we get that much ice? And then... *How did we lose that much ice?*

Answer... WE DON'T KNOW. There are many good theories, but in the final analysis no one is certain of all the dynamics causing our cooling and warming.

The second, the Cryogenian Ice Age, was perhaps the most severe of all. It was dubbed "Snowball Earth." It started about 800 million years ago and covered Earth's entire surface with ice. Glaciers at the equator we're estimated to be eighteen to twenty kilometers thick!

Again... How could we get that much ice, *and how did we get rid of it?* Same answer as before... WE DON'T KNOW. Though many theories are offered, no one knows with certainty.

Virtually everything we know about Earth's Ice Ages is gained through Geological study of what the glaciers leave behind when they recede. As they grow and advance, they grind down hills, gouge up boulders and rocks and soil, and take virtually everything that's in their path. As they melt and recede, they leave behind ridges of sediment, with all that they've "bulldozed" and ground-up. This is the evidence Geologists and others study. Additional geological evidence is found in rock scouring and scratching and valley cutting by the glaciers.

The third, the Andean-Saharan Ice Age, occurred about 450 million years ago, and began shortly after the evolution of land plants and an increase in the planetary oxygen level. Glaciers covered most of what is now Africa and South America.

The fourth Ice Age began about 350 million years ago, and came during a period of massive increase in the evolving plant life around the planet.

The last major Ice Age, the Quaternary Ice Age, started about 2½ million years ago. It formed the Arctic ice cap, and added to the Antarctic ice cap and Greenland's ice sheet. That Ice Age ended about 17,000 years ago.

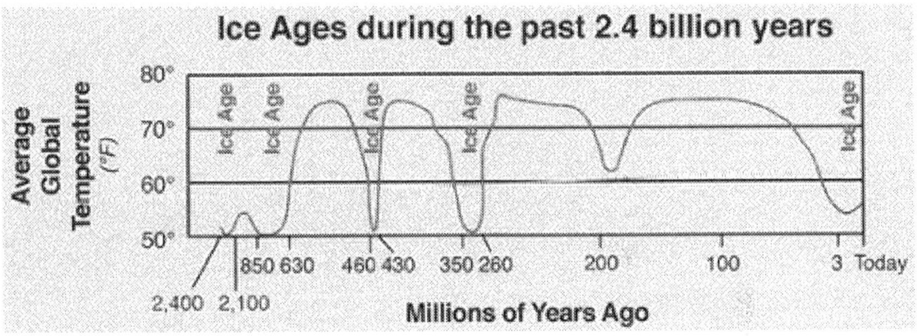

Ice cores and layers of dolomite show that during some glacial periods we've had levels of CO_2 in the atmosphere as high as 12%. Our current level is 0.04%. (Many Scientists contend Earth is currently CO_2 starved.) How could we have **12% CO_2** levels in the atmosphere and not have runaway, through-the-roof global warming. Many Climate Scientists contend that's because CO_2 doesn't *cause* warming.

Throughout the five Ice Ages, there have been numerous glacial periods happening in roughly 40,000 and 100,000 year cycles, with warm, interglacial periods between. It is thought that these glacial and interglacial cycles are largely due to the variations in Earth's orbit and the tilt of its axis.

Serbian mathematician, Milutin Milankovitch, concluded the glacial cycles were influenced by Earth's orbital variations, eccentricity, and procession; plus its axial tilt, ***which all affect solar radiation levels that reach the Earth's surface.***

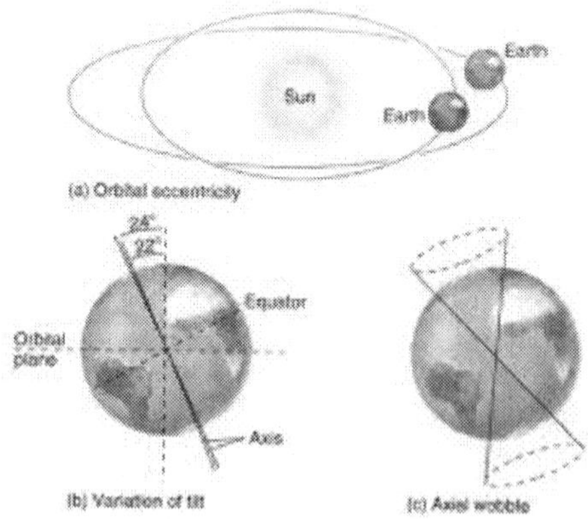

Illustration of Milankovitch's Orbital Variations, Axial Tilt and Procession.

The "Milankovitch Cycles" defined these three major variations:

*Eccentricity - The changes in Earth's orbit cycle over a 100,000 year period. It slowly changes from a near circular orbit to an elliptical one, then back.

*Obliquity - The tilt of the Earth's axis ranges from 22° to 24.5°, and transitions over about a 40,000 year cycle.

*Precession - The wobbling movement of the Earth's axis as it rotates. The axis rotates in a circular pattern over a 26,000 year period.

The action of all three of these systems can create situations where, when everything is lined up in the right manner, the sun will provide the least amount of solar radiation to a large area of Earth. This would cause cooling and even an ice age. And the opposite would also be true with warming.

Obviously, the Milankovitch Cycles are not the only factor affecting climate change. Other factors would include oceans, water vapor, clouds, precipitation, soil-moisture, Southern Oscillations, South Pacific Convergence, North Atlantic Oscillations, El Niño, Intertropical Convergence, the Hadley Circulation, Madden-Julian Oscillations, atmospheric blocking, tropical cyclones, storm tracks, jet streams, etc. (But the disciples of "Man-Made Global Warming" say it's ONLY our CO_2 emissions.)

The most recent glaciation Earth has experienced is known as the "Little Ice Age," beginning in the early 16th century and ending in the mid-19th century. Obviously, weather records weren't being kept at that time, but there is an abundance of proxy and anecdotal evidence showing the extreme winters they experienced.

So, we've had extended warm periods, Ice Ages, glacial and interglacial periods, with average global temperatures varying **7°C colder** to **12°C warmer** than today's average. We've recorded Earth's highest temperature in modern history of 58°C (136°F) and the coldest at -88°C (-126°F). Meanwhile, for two decades, we've had Al Gore and his loyal "Warmists" promoting *extreme alarmism* because, "The climate has warmed **0.**8°C during the last century. And it's *our fault*."

A Brief Look at Earth's Recent Climate Changes

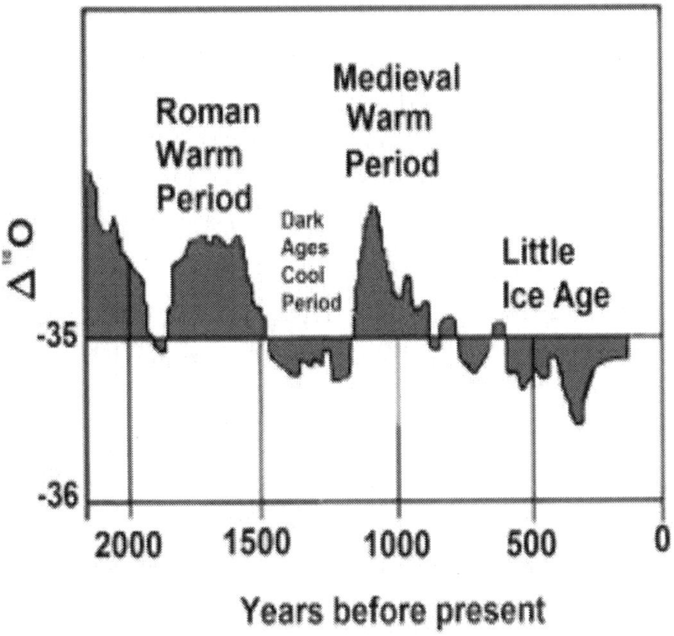

There have been four significant changes in Earth's climate in the last two thousand years:

1. The Roman Warm Period
2. The Dark Ages Cold Period
3. The Medieval Warm Period
4. The Little Ice Age

The Roman Warm Period started about the year 200 BC and lasted about 400 years.

The Dark Ages Cold Period started about 450 AD and lasted until about 850 AD.

The Medieval Warm Period began around 1000 AD and lasted roughly 350 years.

And the Little Ice Age began about 1500 and ended in the mid-1800s.

There is more than ample *proxy* (indirect records of ancient climatic conditions, such as ice cores, cores of lake sediment, and the annual growth rings in trees) and anecdotal evidence of these climate cycles. STILL, the Climatistas (leaders and followers of the IPCC and their Man-Made Global Warming theory) *have made numerous attempts to erase them from the record.*

Why would they want to do that?

Because they can't explain these warm periods when there were no man-made CO_2 emissions to point at and blame. Nor can they refer to the current warming as "unprecedented," and "warmer than it's ever been." The Climatistas have attempted to "adjust" global temperature records in every area possible, always to the benefit of their Man-Made Warming argument.

A Brief Look at the Environmental Movement

In the 1960s, the “Greens” began using, and then ramping-up as much as possible, *scare tactics* to influence public policy. The first Eco-scare was the "Pesticide Scare." In particular, it was banning the use of DDT by the EPA in 1972. The primary reasoning for the ban was the alleged effect on the egg shells of eagles and other raptors, leading to thinner shells and putting the raptors at risk for survival. This was later proven false and shown that the raptor’s egg shells had been thinning long before the use of DDT.

Through the late 1970s and into the 1980s there were many high level discussions among “Environmentalists” about the use of **“Global Warming” or *“Climate Change” as an excellent vehicle to accomplish a variety of agendas*.**” Among the early leaders of these discussions was Bert Bolin. He was an advisor to the prime minister of Sweden, and became the *first head of the IPCC.*

The next scare was "Acid Rain" during the late 1970s. The ***"Settled Science"*** (a term used a couple of key times by the “environmentalists,” like in the current reference to Global Warming) showed that coal fired power plants produced too much sulfur dioxide and carbon dioxide causing acid rain, the acidification of lakes, the destruction of fish, and the destruction of forests.

Their *"Settled Science"* eventually fell apart when it was found that not only is rain naturally acidic, rain had not caused the acidification of lakes or the destruction of forests. Scientists instead found that the change of land use had caused those lakes to become more acidic, resulting in the loss of game fish in the lakes, particularly in the Adirondacks. The EPA knew this long before fraudulently pushing its Clean Air Act *Amendments of 1990.*

Next came the "Ozone Depletion" scare, which stated, "Depleting the ozone would lead to higher incidence of skin cancer and eye damage, and potential climate disaster." UNEP's (United Nations Environmental Program) 1994 Assessment was found to have *greatly overestimated* the "human caused ozone depletion."

Then we come to the Disaster of all disasters... Scare of all scares... "Man-Made Global Warming."

In the beginning...

The IPCC's reliability was crippled at its birth.

The organization was first formed by the UNFCCC (United Nations Framework Convention on Climate Change) and was given **a *mandate* to define climate change as human-caused and to *disregard* any natural causes for climate change.** This essentially predetermined all of the IPCC's *"scientific conclusions."*

The organization was tasked with *finding a human impact on climate*, and then to call upon all nations of the world to do something about it. And the organization pursued this mandate with a fierce dedication, and the knowledge that ***"control a nation's energy and you control the nation."***

In their first Comprehensive Assessment Report of 1990, the IPCC summarized its findings in this interesting statement:

"**The observed 20th century temperature increase could be largely due to natural variability**."

Consider that statement. In effect they concluded natural variability – "Mother Nature" - is the likely cause of the warming, just as she has been with climate change for about two billion years.

Since that first report, the IPCC has continually ramped up its efforts to "strengthen" their position, until now they present statements such as:

"**It is extremely likely that human activity has caused more than half of the observed increase in global temperatures.**"

Extremely likely... More than half... These are statements of ***opinion*** not of scientific findings from research and experimentation.

Each subsequent report and public statement has become more **alarming and dramatic**, now with titles such as:

"We Have Limited Time to Act."

"We have only 12 years to limit the climate change catastrophe."

What evidence exists that increased CO2 from human activity causes global warming? **NONE!** No scientific proof has ever been demonstrated.

"Man-Made Global Warming is a theory for which there is no scientific proof," *says Ecologist and co-founder of Greenpeace, Patrick Moore.*

That's why the IPCC and its disciples deal in statements such as, "highly likely, compelling, very confident" and so on. These are statements of ***opinion,*** not fact.

Global Warming isn't a scientific debate. It's a political debate. It's the latest, and most deceitful, "crisis du jour" of the environmental movement.

Their "science" offers as proof, their unreliable Global Climate Models (GMCs). These models prove themselves to be **consistently inaccurate** when analyzed against the actual temperature results, while the models are constantly tweaked, adjusted, and modified.

A Brief Look at Climate Models.

Global Climate Models (GCMs) have never proven themselves accurate in predicting future climate. With decades of programmers and researchers working to improve the ability of GCMs to more accurately simulate climate, the models still fail to match actual outcomes. That is primarily due to the difficulty in simulating all of the various elements that affect Earth's climate continually.

The IPCC touts their computer models, and the use of physics to calculate how energy flows into, through, and out of Earth's land, water, and atmosphere. More than 100 such models have been created and are frequently used today to make extremely dire predictions about the fate of our planet. The problem is that the models have serious flaws and limitations that drastically limit their value in making predictions and in guiding governmental policy making. Three primary short-comings are described below. Each one alone is enough to make one doubt the predictions. All three together should deal a devastating blow to the idea of relying on the models to accurately forecast climate or make predictions.

1. Measurement Error

When the size of what you are measuring is smaller than the size of the margin of error. Scientists present "measurement error" or "margin of error" by the range around the pertinent measurement. For example, they say that a temperature is 20°C ±0.5°C. The temperature is very likely to be 20.0°C, but it could reasonably be as high as 20.5°C or as low as 19.5°C.

Now consider the temperatures that are recorded by weather stations around the world. They contend, "...the 1880–2004 increase in global temperature is 0.80°C ± 0.98°C." The margin of error is larger than the increase in temperature they were trying to determine.

2. The Sun's Energy

Climate models are used to assess the CO_2 global warming hypothesis and to quantify the human-caused CO_2 "footprint." If their estimate of the sun's energy in model simulations were off by as little as 0.01% (one-one hundredth of a percent), that error would swamp the estimated extra energy from any human CO_2 emissions. Unfortunately, the sun is just of many uncertainties they have.

3. Cloud Errors

Clouds reflect incoming radiation and also trap it as it is outgoing. A world entirely encompassed by clouds would have dramatically different atmospheric temperatures than one devoid of clouds. But modeling clouds and their effects has proven extremely difficult. The IPCC acknowledged this in their *Assessment Report* from 2013: "***The simulation of clouds in climate models remains challenging.***"

Some of the other elements that can affect global climate, and are not accurately represented in computer models, are: Water vapor, precipitation, solar radiation, oceans, soil-moisture, biological processes, permafrost, the Milankovitch Cycles, Southern Oscillation, North Atlantic Oscillation, South Pacific Convergence, intertropical convergence, the Hadley Circulation, El Niño, Madden-Julian Oscillation, atmospheric blocking, tropical cyclone, jet streams, etc.

Dozens of separate scientific disciplines make up "Climate Science." Few Scientists are expert in more than two of these disciplines. They include Geology, Geochronology, Geochemistry, Sedimentology, Glaciology, Tectonics, Paleontology, Climatology, Archaeology, Geophysics, Ecology, Astronomy, Oceanography, Solar Physics, Meteorology and, by some estimates, 60 or 70 more.

The following graph depicts:

(1) Satellite temperature measurements with a connected line of squares.

(2) Weather balloon measurements in the line of round dots.

(3) The average of over one hundred of the GCM predictions is depicted by the bold line.

The prediction of warming by the models always exceeds the actual recorded data, and that difference is always magnified with increased time parameters.

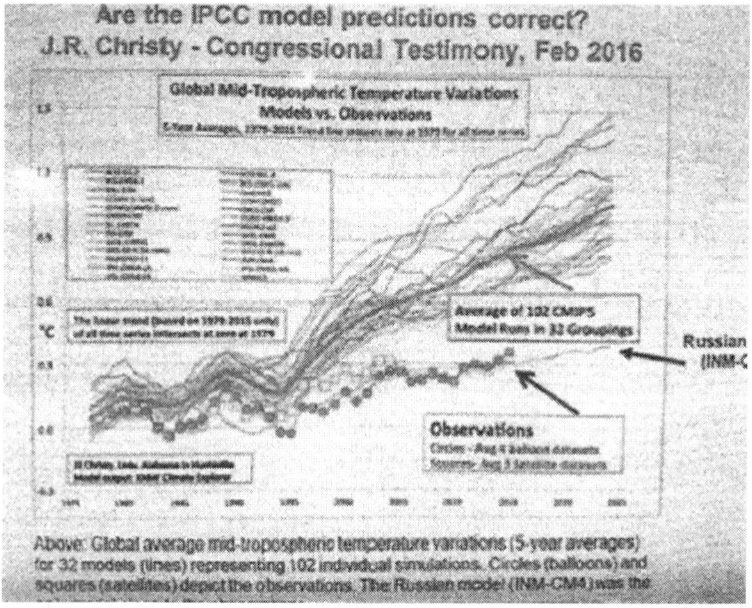

AND, *modelers* (in support of the IPCC's position) *exclude some elements that run counter to the mission of finding human influence on climate.*

A Brief Look at the "97% Consensus"

There is no consensus among Climate Scientists regarding global warming or climate change. The surveys that are most commonly used in support of the "97% Consensus" are, ***without exception***, flawed and deliberately misleading. Most *working scientists* disagree with the IPCCs claim of such a consensus. Science is not done by consensus.

The first study proclaiming the "97% Consensus" was done in 2009 by University of Illinois masters student, Kendall Zimmerman and her adviser, Peter Doran. Based on a two-question online survey (sent to more than 10,000 members of the American Geophysical Union), Zimmerman and Doran concluded that, on the subject of global warming and the role played by human activity, ***the debate is over.*** Of the 3100 scientists that responded to their survey, only 5% (or 160) of the respondents were Climate Scientists.

Then the "**97%**" was achieved by drawing from an even smaller subset. ***They hand-picked 77 of the responders*** *(who had a self-interest) "who were self-reported climate scientists, and who had more than 50% of their recently published peer-reviewed papers written on the subject of climate change."*

Of these 77 hand-picked scientists, 75 agreed that *"Global temperatures have risen since 1900 and that human activity is the significant contributing factor."*

75 out of 77... Voila... "97% Consensus."

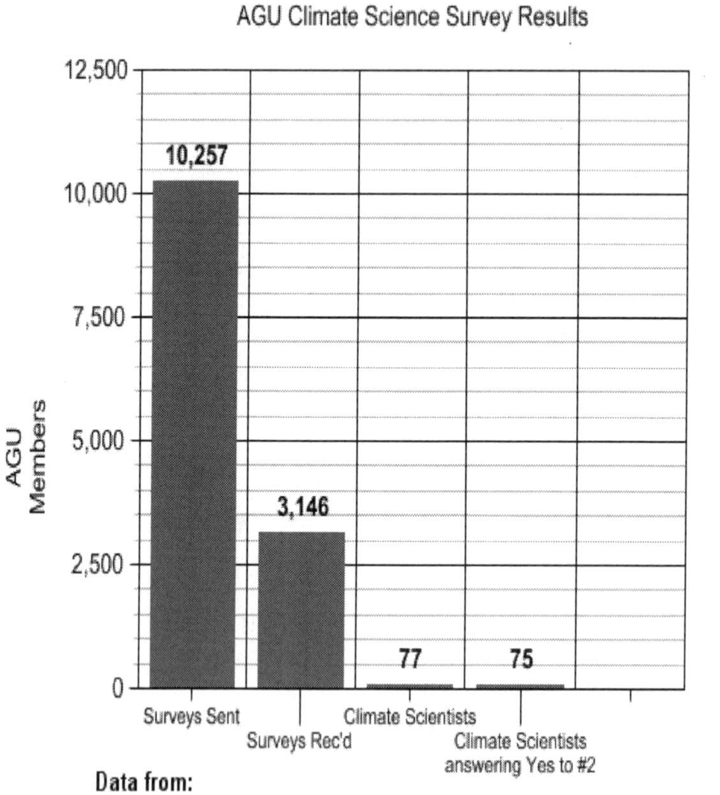

Data from:
Doran, P. T. and M. K. Zimmerman (2009), Examining the Scientific Consensus on Climate Change, Eos Trans. AGU, 90(3), 22, doi: 10.1029/2009EO030002.

(Several other "surveys" are just as vacuous.)

A Brief Look at the NIPCC

The NIPCC (Nongovernmental International Panel on Climate Change) is an organization established by the *S. Fred Singer Science & Environmental Policy Project* in direct opposition to the assessment reports of the Intergovernmental Panel on Climate Change (IPCC), particularly on the issue of man-made global warming.

NIPCC states that their purpose is to objectively analyze and interpret data *without a specific agenda.* Unlike the IPCC, which they contend is *government-sponsored, politically motivated, and predisposed to believing that climate change is not debatable, and that it is a problem in need of a United Nations solution.*

The NIPCC contends Earth's temperature, over its long history, has fluctuated from -7°C to +12°C (compared to the twentieth century average temperature). A predicted warming of 1.2°C, should it occur this century, falls well within the bounds of *natural variability* and not a "*crisis.*"

NIPCC also contends that, with the current level of 405 ppm, we still live in a CO2-starved world. All life on earth is dependent on CO2.

The overall warming since 1850 represents our recovery from the Little Ice Age. Earth has not warmed significantly *for the last two decades,* despite the continuing, significant increase in atmospheric CO_2 levels.

<u>IPCC</u> cites the following as *evidence* of the Man-Made Global Warming Theory:

1. Unusual melting is occurring in mountain glaciers, Arctic sea ice, and polar ice-caps.

2. Global sea level is rising at an enhanced rate and swamping tropical coral reefs.

3. The intensity of droughts, floods, and monsoons is increasing.

4. Warming is leading to more intense wildfires, rainfall, storms, hurricanes, and other extreme weather events.

NIPCC's response to the IPCC's "*evidence*":

1. The continuous melting of Arctic sea ice, polar ice-caps and glaciers ***is not occurring at an "unnatural" rate*** and does not constitute evidence of a human impact on the climate. Glaciers and ice caps have and will continue to melt since we came out of the Little Ice Age.

2. Data shows that sea-level rise is not accelerating. Local and regional sea levels continue to exhibit natural variability. Overall, sea levels continue to rise at the same rate that they have since we began keeping records.

3. No relationship has been proven between climate warming over the past 100 years and an increase in extreme weather events.

4. Historical records show that there is *no significant increase in the number of, or the intensity of, rainstorms, hurricanes, tornadoes or any other extreme weather events.* (IN fact, Meteorological Science suggests just the opposite: A warmer world will see milder weather patterns.)

The NIPCC contends that the IPCC's Global Climate Models – *which comprise the backbone of their argument for Man-Made Global Warming* – are exceedingly flawed. They do not accurately account for water vapor, which is the dominant green-house gas and much more influential than CO2. Nor do they accurately account for solar radiation or clouds. They argue that the 0.0016% of CO2 that is increased in the atmosphere from human activity has more influence on our climate than water vapor, clouds, and the sun's radiation.

I repeat... They argue that the 0.0016% of our atmosphere that is *the CO2 increase resulting from human activity* (one molecule of CO2 in every 85,000 molecules of the atmosphere) has more influence on our climate than water vapor, clouds, and the sun's radiation.

This has resulted in forecasts made by the GCMs that are proven wrong by actual data on a regular basis. While there has been negligible warming between 1998 and 2018, virtually all (more than 100 GCMs) of the models predicted warming between 0.**30**°C and 0.**70**°C. By comparison, Earth's climate actually warmed 0.**07**°C during those 20 years.

A Brief Look at Climategate

"Climategate" began in November 2009, when a whistle-blower leaked nearly a thousand emails, central to a 'Freedom of Information' request placed with the Climatic Research Unit of the University of East Anglia in the United Kingdom.

Then, two years later, a new batch of nearly 5,000 emails between scientists central to the "*human caused global warming crisis*" were released to the public, igniting another firestorm.

In these emails, exchanged between the prominent scientists of the "warming movement," they discussed 1) *Efforts to exclude "skeptics and deniers" from publishing in journals; 2) Punish editors who allowed denier articles to appear in their journal; 3) Stonewall requests for original data; 4) Manipulate the data used; 5) Rush into publication all articles refuting or attempting to discredit scientists who disagree with IPCC's position."*

Global Warming and its cause is a valid question, of ultimate global importance. A concern that most people would have thought should have ***demanded*** *the most careful, exacting and rigorous scientific analyses that mankind could muster.*

Instead of seeing large collaborations of meticulous, careful, critical scientists, ***Climategate*** gave us a peephole into the work of a small team of "scientists" building a wall around themselves and their fellow activists, to prevent real scientists from seeing the their questionable research data. "Global Warming" became a *Movement* in search of the huge and continuous funding available from governments around the world, and is antithetical to science itself.

Three themes emerged from the released emails:

(1) Prominent scientists central to the global warming debate were taking measures to conceal rather than disseminate underlying data.

(2) These scientists, unfortunately, view global warming as purely a ***"cause"*** rather than a balanced scientific inquiry.

(3) Many of the emails admit their *science is weak* and dependent on *deliberate manipulation of data.*

Scientific transparency, a defining characteristic of the Scientific Method, is the "Open sharing of scientific data, methods, theories and procedures so that independent parties (especially skeptics) of a particular hypothesis can ***replicate and validate*** asserted observations." Emails between Climategate scientists, however, show a concerted effort to hide rather than disseminate underlying evidence, data, and procedures.

The following is a sampling of the emails:

"Any work that we have done is done on the back of the research grants we get and has to be well hidden." (Phil Jones, Director of Climate Research.)

"The trick is to decide on the main message of our report, and then determine what we will let in and what we will keep out." writes Jonathan Overpeck, lead author for IPCC's climate assessment report.

"I gave up on her (Georgia Institute of Technology Climate Professor, Judith Curry) a while ago. I don't know what she thinks she's doing, but it's not helping ***the cause***," wrote Michael Mann (creator of the discredited Hockey Stick chart).

"I have been talking w/folks about finding an investigative journalist to ***investigate and expose McIntyre*** (Climate Skeptic Steve McIntyre), Mann writes in another email.

Tom Wigley, scientist at the University Corporation for Atmospheric Research, asserted they "must get rid of the editor of a peer-reviewed science journal because he published some papers contradicting assertions of the global warming crisis."

"There remain significant errors in the simulation of clouds, which likely contribute to erroneous predictions by the models."

"Mike, the Figure you sent is excellent. Very deceptive. <u>There have been more than a few dishonest model results by authors and by the IPCC,</u>" Wigley acknowledges.

* * *

More than revealing misconduct, the emails reveal the frank admission of the scientific shortcomings of their Man Made Global Warming assertions.

And don't forget for a moment that the entire industry of "Global Warming" was created out of virtually nothing just to get the massive, available government funding. Funding that was almost universally one-sided in its requirement that its recipients find evidence for *man-made climate change*, rather than investigate the possibility that other factors could have caused the warming.

Many "climate scientists" have built their entire career on this funding. So, it is not surprising that they became completely dependent on its conditional lifeline, and they've single-mindedly focused on achieving the ends for which they were commissioned – and would attack any intruders or interlopers who threatened it.

A Brief Look at the "Hockey Stick."

"Climate scientists" with the IPCC for the last three decades have attempted to adjust, amend, correct, modify, or just fraudulently change climate records. In my opinion, one of the most egregious of these is Michael Mann's (discredited) hockey stick graph. Mann, "adjusted" climate records to show a relatively flat temperature line with 1,000 years of slight cooling until about 1950. *Then comes the sudden, radical warming period, "all due to CO2 emissions from human activity."*

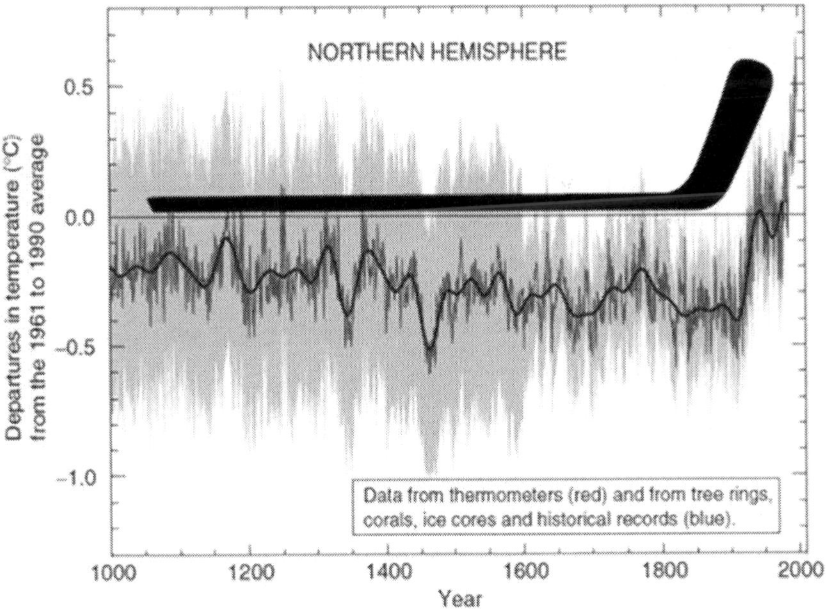

How convenient. No explanation needed for the Medieval Warm Period (where there was no "carbon footprint" to blame). AND, no explanation needed for how it cooled. AND, now the door was open to refer to the current warming as "unprecedented."

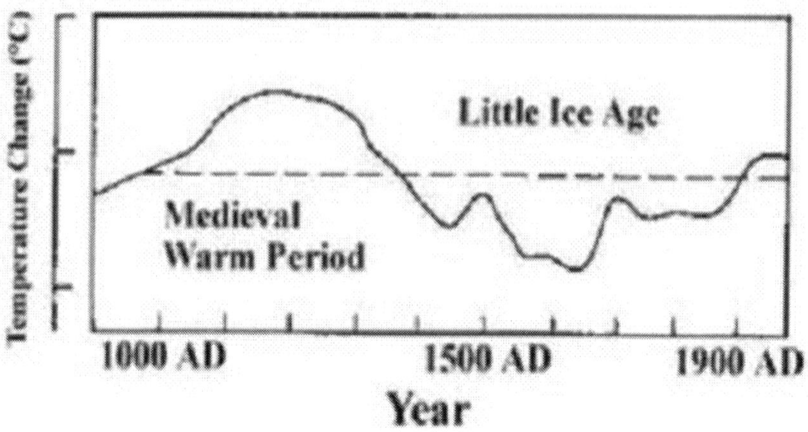

Graph from 1990 IPCC Report

This chart from the IPCC's 1990 Report shows the two periods, roughly 300 years in length: The Medieval Warm Period and The Little Ice Age. They had temperature variations much greater than anything we've experienced the last 100 years. Compare this with Mann's "reconstruction" that basically flattens the temperatures so that it shows an overall trend of "cooling" until 1950. Then we see the "unprecedented" warming (naturally due to CO2 emissions from human activity).

U.S. Senate Committee on Environment & Public Works
Hearing Statements

Date: 12/06/2006

Statement of Dr. David Deming
University of Oklahoma
College of Earth and Energy
Climate Change and the Media

Mr. Chairman, members of the Committee, and distinguished guests, thank you for inviting me to testify today. I am a geologist and geophysicist. I have a bachelor's degree in geology from Indiana University, and a Ph.D in geophysics from the University of Utah. My field of specialization in geophysics is temperature and heat flow. In recent years, I have turned my studies to the history and philosophy of science. In 1995, I published a short paper in the academic journal Science. In that study, I reviewed how borehole temperature data recorded a warming of about one degree Celsius in North America over the last 100 to 150 years. The week the article appeared, I was contacted by a reporter for National Public Radio. He offered to interview me, but only if I would state that the warming was due to human activity. When I refused to do so, he hung up on me.

I had another interesting experience around the time my paper in Science was published. I received an astonishing email from a major researcher in the area of climate change. He said, "We have to get rid of the Medieval Warm Period."

The Medieval Warm Period (MWP) was a time of unusually warm weather that began around 1000 AD and persisted until a cold period known as the "Little Ice Age" took hold in the 14th century. Warmer climate brought a remarkable flowering of prosperity, knowledge, and art to Europe during the High Middle Ages.

The existence of the MWP had been recognized in the scientific literature for decades. But now it was a major embarrassment to those maintaining that the 20th century warming was truly anomalous. It had to be "gotten rid of."

In the memo above, using "U.S Senate Committee on Environment & Public Works" letterhead, Dr. David Deming tells of a request, *"To get rid of the Medieval Warm Period."*

Mann used tree rings to do a "proxy reconstruction" of climate records for the past thousand years. Mark Steyn said of Mann's work, "There are only two problems with his work... The proxies and the reconstruction."

Amazingly, the new record of temperatures exactly fits the rise in CO_2, the IPCC's climate theory, and their GCMs (models).

Stephen McIntyre was suspicious and sought to verify Mann's work. However, Mann refused to provide his data or methods – a basic requirement of any scientific paper. It required legal action to finally pry the information loose from Mann's grip. It took McIntyre only days to discredit the work.

McIntyre contended that Mann's statistics were so flawed that you could input random data (even stock prices) and still have a result similar to the hockey stick nine times out of ten.

More examples of "data adjusting" are on the next two pages.

Jim Hansen – The Climate Chiropractor. Need some temperatures adjusted? Call Dr. James Hansen. (You can do so much cool stuff when you control the historical record.) But, in 1999, Dr. James Hansen made these remarkable comments:

"Empirical evidence does not lend much support to the notion that climate is headed swiftly toward more extreme heat and drought.

"In the U.S. there has been little temperature change in the past 50 years, at a time of rapidly increasing greenhouse gases — in fact, there was a slight cooling throughout most of the country."

GISS US temperature data showed an 80+ year decline in US temperature averages, with 1934, 1921 and 1931 being the three hottest years.

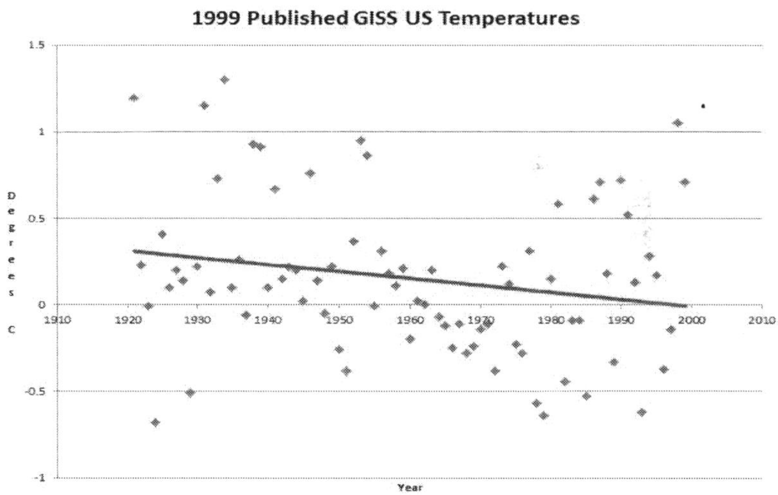

Hansen's comments and graph have been deleted from the GISS web site, but originally resided there.

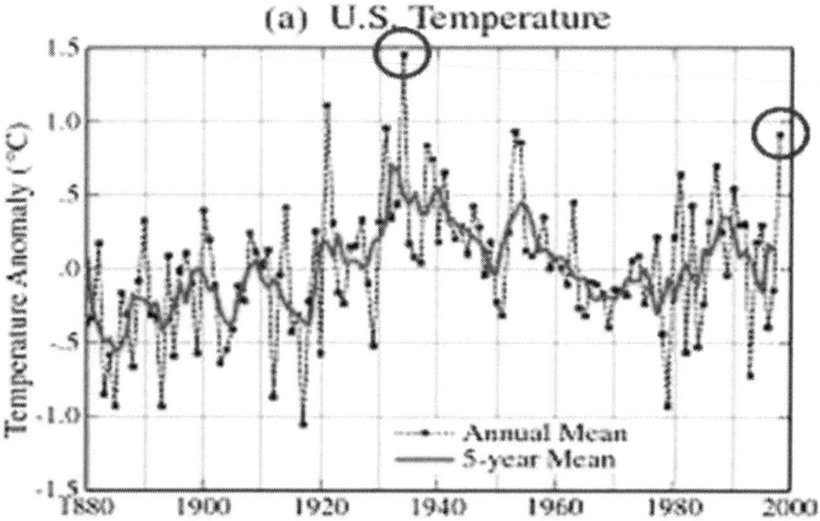

NASA's chart showing our warmest temperatures in the 1930s... Before making "necessary" adjustments to correct the records. Amazingly, their "new and improved" chart shows higher temperatures in 1998 and later, and conveniently fits the CO2 Dogma. As the Church Lady would say, *"Well isn't that special."* (New chart is below.)

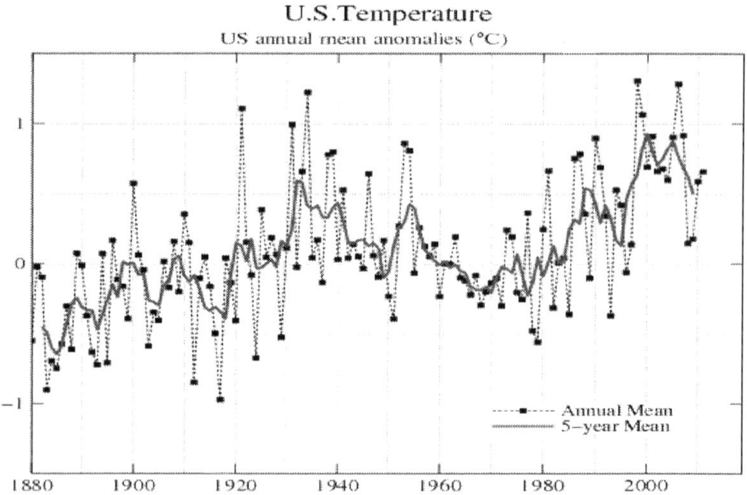

A Brief Look at the Scientific Method and Political Science

In direct contradiction to the "Scientific Method," the IPCC *assumes its hypothesis is correct*, and that it's only duty is to collect evidence and make arguments in favor of that hypothesis.

The IPCC expresses "great confidence" in its assumptions, but cannot apply a statistical level because they are all statements of opinion, *not of provable fact.*

In all of the websites supporting Man-Made Global Warming, terms like: Compelling... Very likely... Highly Confident... are used repeatedly. *Again, these are statements of opinion, not of scientific fact as a result of experimentation.*

Criticism of the IPCC has not only come from individual scientists. **Nature**, a prominent science journal, editorialized in 2013: ***"It's time to rethink the IPCC. Their current report should be its last mega-assessment."*** (Nature, 2013)

Particularly harsh criticism came from the Amsterdam-based ***Inter-Academy Council (IAC).*** This council is made up of the Presidents of many of the world's national science academies. They conducted a thorough audit of IPCC and found the following:

Fake confidence levels: IAC was highly critical of IPCC's method of assigning "confidence" levels to its findings and forecasts.

Use of grey-sources: Overuse and reliance upon unpublished and non-peer-reviewed sources.

Political interference: Late-night, line-by-line editing of already approved reports.

Use of secret data: An unwillingness to share data and respond to freedom-of-information requests.

Selection of contributors far too politicized: Government politicians decide which scientist are allowed take part in the writing and review process.

The Scientific Method involves several basic, universal steps:

*A Question or Observation

*Construct a Hypothesis

*Test with Experimentation

*Analysis & Skepticism

*Conclusion:

Results align with Hypothesis - Report

Results don't align with Hypothesis –
More work and re-testing needed.

*Share data and communicate results.

When *politics* ***supplanted*** *science* in the realm of global warming, you had politicians, environmental activist, and fund seeking groups (primarily in the Renewable Energy industry) repeatedly quoting the IPCC's alarming claims and predictions. And, over time, <u>they began removing the important qualifying statements in which the IPCC expressed any doubts or reservations.</u>

Rather than object to this mishandling of its work, the IPCC liked and began to encourage it. Over time all news releases became more and more alarmist. Soon, many of the IPCC news releases were influenced and/or written by the professional environmental activists who had effectively taken over the organization.

Stephan Schneider, Professor of Environmental Biology and strong IPCC supporter, wrote, "To reduce the risk of losing our hold on 'Disastrous Climate Change,' we need to capture the public's imagination. So, we have to offer up scary scenarios, make dramatic statements, make no mention of doubts, and **find the right balance between** ***<u>being honest and being effective."</u>***

Michael Hulme, Professor of Climate at King's College London, and a former Professor of Climate Change at the University of East Anglia wrote, *"We will continue to create, tell and write new and alarming stories about Climate Change."* He also suggested that fellow Alarmists, *"Keep beating the drum and telling the stories."*

When politics gets involved, many unfortunate circumstances come into play. Such is the case with the **EPA's outright lying** when they stated, "Marine species are shifting northward as air and water temperatures increase. Species such as pollock, halibut, soul, and snow crab are shifting northward due to the warming affecting fisheries of the Bering Sea." They referenced Meuter and Litzow, 2007.

In their 2007 paper, Meuter and Litzow wrote: "The northward displacement of various species is unrelated to temperature or any other climate parameter."

A Brief Look at Global Warming Myths

Myth 1: "Global temperatures have risen at a rapid, unprecedented rate."

The surface temperature index since we began record keeping, shows cyclical warming and cooling periods as follows: a warming trend through the period ending in 1880; then a cooling period through 1911; then warming through 1941; then cooling through 1978; then warming through 1998; then a period of no significant change through 2018. ***There has been no catastrophic warming in the 140 years of Earth's recorded weather history.***

Myth 2: "The 'hockey stick' graph proves Earth has had a steady temperature decrease for more than 1000 years, then, in 1950, began a sudden, dramatic increase due to mankind's CO2 emissions."

Significant changes in climate have been occurring throughout Earth's history such as the **"Medieval Warm Period"** from around 1000 to 1350 AD, followed by the **"Little Ice Age"** which lasted about 300 years.

Since the mid-19th Century, average global temperatures have risen at a slow, steady rate. Although the cooling period from 1941 - 1971 was significant enough that it became a *"Global Cooling & Pending Ice Age"* scare (led by the Environmental Movement).

The "hockey stick" graph tried to erase the Medieval Warm Period and the Little Ice Age. It was later discredited and shown to be extremely flawed and unreliable.

Myth 3: "Human emissions of CO2 has increased greatly over the last hundred years, causing Earth's warming."

CO2 levels have increased significantly during the past hundred years for various reasons – human causes (3% of all CO2 emissions) and natural causes (97% of all CO2 emissions). Ice cores, which preserve the measure of climate and change over hundreds of thousands of years, show that *CO2 levels rose and fell* ***after*** the temperature has done so – usually lagging decades and even more behind the temperature changes. ***Thus the CO2 is influenced by warming, not the cause of warming.***

Myth 4: "<u>Climate Models verify that CO2 increase will cause global warming.</u>"

Computer models used in <u>predicting climate change</u> are examples of "<u>circular reasoning</u>." They can be made to produce any desired outcome by simply adjusting the parameters of input. ***The point is, they do not <u>prove or verify</u> anything***. *Computer models used by the IPCC do not fully allow for, and thus are incapable of properly measuring and predicting the effects of the sun, volcanos, clouds, and water vapor that have a major impact on the Earth's climate.*

The following graph depicts temperatures (the Flat Line) for the last 18 years, and the average CO2 emissions (the rising line) over the same period. ***Increased CO2 did not cause warming.***

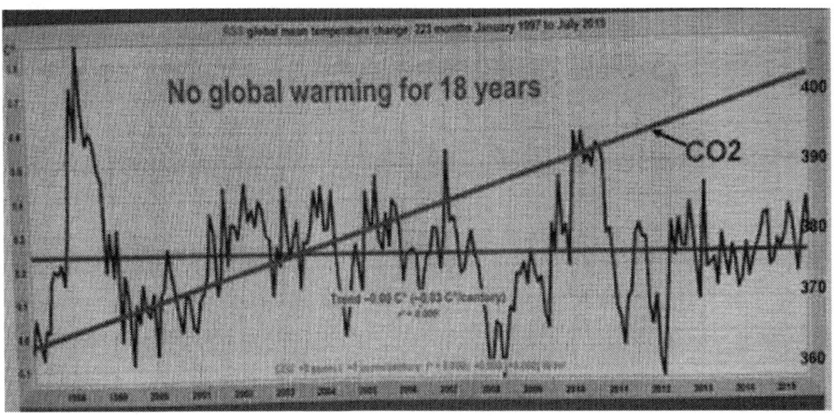

Myth 5: "The IPCC has proven that man-made CO2 is causing global warming."

In the 1996 report from the IPCC, two highly important statements were ***deleted*** from the final draft that was approved by the Panel. They were:

1.) **"None of the studies in this report has shown clear evidence that we can attribute the climate changes to increased levels of greenhouse gases."**

2.) **"None of the studies in this report has attributed warming as being man-made."**

Myth 6: "CO2 is a major pollutant."

Absolutely not true. CO2 is essential for the growth of all plant life and thus it is necessary to all life on Earth. Our atmosphere is comprised of 78% nitrogen and 21% oxygen. The ***remaining 1%*** is comprised of trace gases – CO2 being less than half of that or about **0.4% of our atmosphere.**

Myth 7: "Receding glaciers and the calving of ice shelves are proof of man-made global warming."

Glaciers have been growing and receding cyclically for hundreds of millions of years. Recent glacier melting is a consequence of a warming period since the Little Ice Age. Glaciers have been receding and ice shelves have been breaking off for the last 200 years during the warming.

Myth 8: "Earth's polar ice caps are melting and will disappear."

The thickness and the surface area of the ice at the poles are as variable as Earth's climate. The warming trend from 1978 through 1998 caused melting, primarily in the Arctic polar region. Recently however, temperatures in the Arctic are similar to those recorded in 1940s, and the area and thickness of the ice is returning to the levels of 1980.

In the Antarctic, temperatures have been steadily cooling on the main continent, and the ice cap is the thickest ever recorded.

As stated earlier, during 80% of Earth's TIME it's been **warmer, wetter, and ice free.** We are currently living in one of the cooler times in Earth's long history. And, hopefully, it will continue to warm at a slow rate.

The IPCC was created to find and disseminate research that shows the *human impact* on global climate; it is agenda-driven, and a political rather than scientific body (and some allege it has become corrupt as well).

The hypothesis implicit in all IPCC writing and reporting is that "dangerous global warming is the result of human-related CO2 emissions." In continual contradiction to the Scientific Method, the IPCC assumes its hypothesis is correct and that its only duty is to collect evidence and make plausible arguments in favor of their hypothesis.

No provable correlation exists between the past 150 years of warming and human-related CO2 emissions.

Neither the rate nor the magnitude of the reported late twentieth century warming (1978-1998) *lay outside normal and natural variability*.

On balance, a warming of even 2°C (more than predicted by the "Warmists") during the twenty-first century would not be a harmful "crisis." It is much more likely that many people of the world would benefit from the warmer climate.

A Brief Look at CO_2
Mother Nature's Plant Food

During the past 150 years, Earth's climate has been warming and we've been putting more CO_2 into the atmosphere. These are both true and they seem to have a correlation. That does not mean there is *causation*. It's like the old trope, "The rise in ice cream cone sales has caused more shark attacks." There is a correlation – ice cream sales go up in the summer, as do shark attacks – but there is no *causation*.

The warming of about 0.8°C during the last 100 years resulted in a more comfortable climate, and gave us greater longevity, prosperity, and personal freedom. So, if CO_2 contributed anything to our warming, I say Hallelujah!

If our climate continues to warm, it may be possible to grow food crops in northern regions of Canada and Russia. These are vast areas that are currently far too cold for agriculture. The cold, nasty climate of the Little Ice Age caused widespread crop failures, famine, and severe population decline. Glaciers advanced southward, over-running towns and farms. Scandinavian records show countless farms destroyed by the advancing glaciers.

Carbon is the basis of all life. CO2 is the source of carbon for all plant life, which is the source of life *all the way up the food chain to us humans.*

In Earth's history, CO2 levels we're far greater than today. In our past, there have also been times when CO2 levels were as low as 180 ppm - a level which is only 30 ppm above the level that photosynthesis ceases, destroying all plant life and, consequently, all life on Earth.

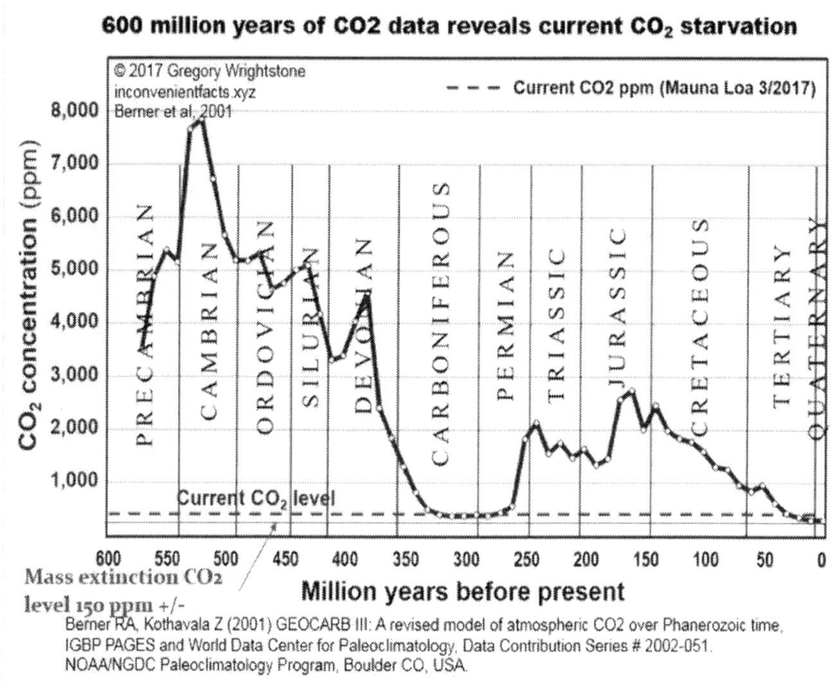

Fortunately, current levels of CO2 are at 405 ppm and Earth has been greening considerably. Satellite photos show new growth in tropical rainforest areas, and sizable shrinking desert areas that are being overtaken by green growth. Crops are flourishing and crop yields are improving, and it's mostly due to the increased level of CO_2. We are nowhere near a level of CO_2 that should be alarming. Scientists estimate the CO_2 in the atmosphere is only 1% of all Earth's CO_2. The remaining 99% is held in the oceans, soils, and rock formations.

Scientists working with ice cores contend that the levels of CO_2 in the atmosphere follow temperature changes, usually lagging behind by decades or more. How does the "Consensus" blatantly and continually ignore this fact and contend that rising global temperatures **are *caused* by our CO_2 emissions.**

The optimum CO_2 level for most plant life is about 1600 ppm, four times higher than today's level. This is why growers purposely pump CO_2 into their greenhouses, resulting in vast increases in yield.

For the past two decades, global CO_2 emissions have increased dramatically with China and India modernizing, building coal-fired power plants, and driving many more cars. During that time, there has been no statistically significant change in Earth's average global temperature. The warming proclaimed by alarmists saying, "...we are setting records," are dealing in *hundredths* of a degree (statistically insignificant) and comparing only to recent temperatures – they don't say that they limit there scope to the last 150 years to be able to fraudulently say "warmest ever," while throughout most of Earth's life it's been warmer then now.

The graph below shows the timeline of Earth's temperature over 2½ billion years. Our current temperature is at the far right. You can see that there have only been a couple of brief times through Earth's history where it's been as cool as we are currently. Throughout history, and even as recent as the Medieval Warm Period, it's been much warmer than today.

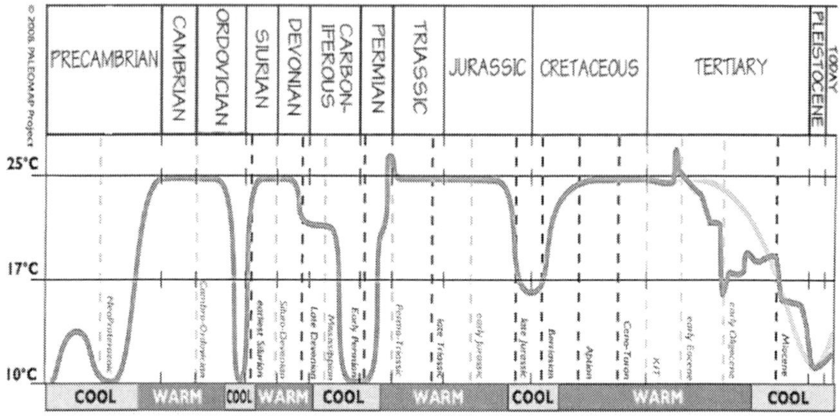

Now, let's look at the Beer-Lambert law. The equation representing the law is straightforward:

A=ebc

Where A is absorbance (no units, since $A = log_{10} P_o / P$) **e** is the absorptivity with units of L mol^{-1} cm^{-1} **b** is the path length **c** is the concentration of the compound in L-1...

(Eyes glazing over.)

In "plain English" it says CO2 absorption of solar radiation and the resulting effect of warming rises until you reach a level of 100 ppm (we are at 405 ppm). <u>After the 100 ppm, there is very little effect when adding more CO2.</u>

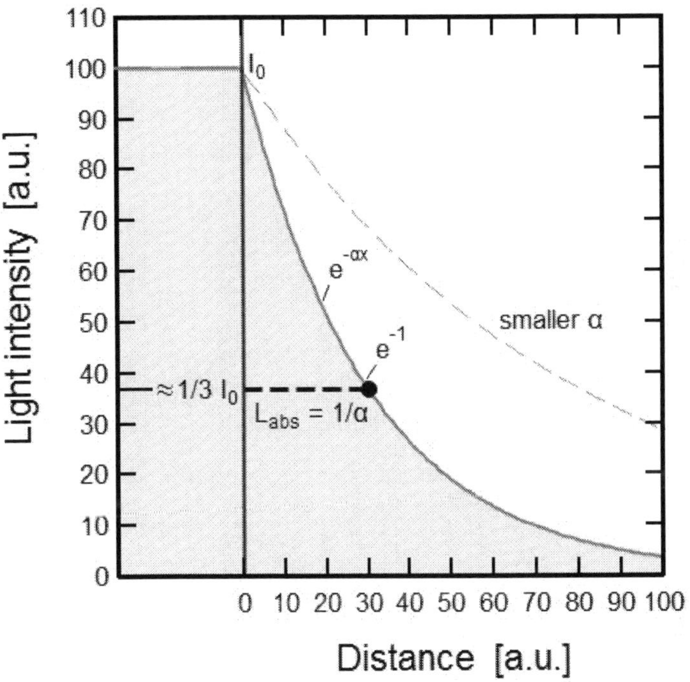

What will happen next with our planet and climate? Warming? Cooling? Who knows? But the guessing, and I'm sure the Alarmism, will continue in heavy doses.

A Brief look at Wikipedia

As mentioned earlier, I was glad that I had printed out most of what I found interesting on Wikipedia 14 years ago. When I finally decided to write this short book (lengthy pamphlet?) of my thoughts on "Warming," I gathered my notes, books, and the file of "copies" on the subject.

As I began organizing the "stuff" and searching Wikipedia for updated material, I was disappointed (but not surprised) that I couldn't find much of what I'd found years before. That which I did find had been rewritten with a bias favoring the "Warmist Theology." Then I ran across a site telling of the "editing" of Wikipedia articles by William Connelly.

A 2009 investigative report from the UK's *Telegraph,* detailed the extent of the powers that Connelly possessed at Wikipedia, allowing him to remove any information that didn't conform to his point of view. With a press of his 'delete' button, more than 500 articles disappeared.

If he disapproved of any of the positions taken by someone, he would have them barred from the site. More than 2,000 contributors found themselves blocked from making any arguments or submissions to the site.

He re-wrote thousands of articles and submissions that he didn't like or didn't agree with. All told, Connelly rewrote or created more than 5,400 Wikipedia articles on Global Warming.

He wiped out any reference to the **1970s Global Cooling Scare**, and then went after *the warmer-than-now* **Medieval Warm Period**. For a time he was on a mission of rewriting virtually all the Wikipedia commentary on the greenhouse effect, making CO2 the dominant issue of global warming, and eliminating anything contrary to the theory.

One example: ***"The climate system is a coupled non-linear, chaotic system and therefore long term predictions of future climate are not possible." IPCC, 2001.*** This IPCC statement was recorded in over 30 different sites on Wikipedia and Google. Now it can be found nowhere... wiped clean... except where they've messaged it to fit their narrative.

Connelly *rewrote articles on global warming, on the greenhouse effect, on the instrumental temperature record, on the urban heat island, on climate models, on global cooling, and on, and on.*

Ultimately, Connelly turned Wikipedia into a missionary wing for all the disciples and acolytes of the global warming movement.

A Brief Look at the 1970s Global Cooling Scare

Time magazine's cover story for June 24, 1974 was "Another Ice Age?"

Newsweek magazine's cover story April 28th, 1975 "The Cooling World."

Time magazine's cover from 1977 was "The Big Freeze."

Kenneth Watt, Ecologist, wrote in 1970, "If present trends continue, the Earth will be about 5°C colder by the year 2000. This is more than enough to put us into another Ice Age."

Some believed there was a "Scientific Consensus" in the 1970s that the Earth was in a period of significant cooling and maybe even heading into the next Ice Age.

The question of whether or not there was a global cooling "Consensus" in the 1970s is important to the Alarmists because, if there was a "Consensus" and it was subsequently proved to be wrong, then it would question the *legitimacy of any consensus in science.* If the "Consensus" was wrong, then how legitimate is a consensus in science?

For most of us that lived through the 1970s, it was the perception that global cooling dominated everything to do with "weather." Some of the winters back then were like living in the Arctic, with brutal and unrelenting cold and blizzards.

And there was some fearmongering over "Global Cooling" also. But as we neared the '80s, it began to warm, and it became evident that, for now, we weren't headed into an Ice Age.

The issue of human-caused CO2 emissions was not a part of the Alarmist Lexicon at that time, but CO2 was significantly higher in the 1960s and 70s then it had been during the 1930s and 40s. So, how could there be a cooling period rather than "global warming."

Then the Environmental Movement, seeing that the people had not been sufficiently panicked by Global Cooling and the possibility of another Ice Age, quickly did an about-face and proclaimed we were headed into catastrophic "Global Warming."

A Brief Look at Earth's Climate History

The graph below represents average temperatures between 1880 and 2010. *Compare* the period 1910 - 1940 to the period 1980 - 2010. They both show roughly the same amount of warming at roughly the same rate. *How could that be?* Between 1910 and 1940 CO2 emissions from human activity was negligible compared to the later period, but the warming was at the same rate and the same magnitude. (Alarmists... Please explain.)

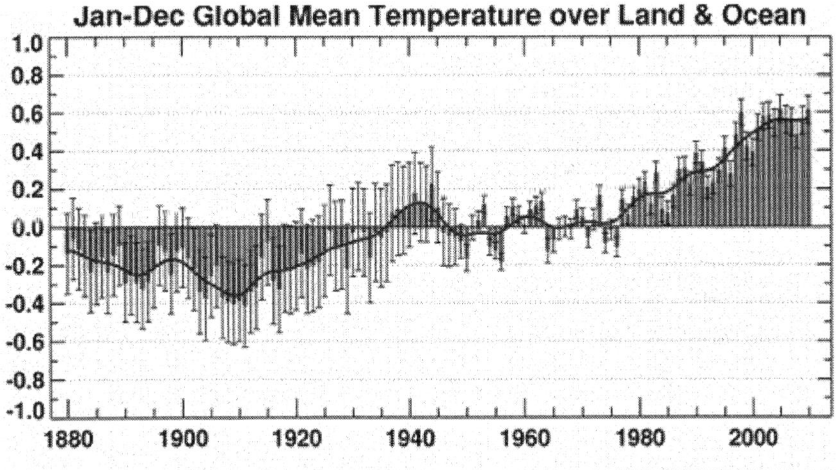

The next graph shows 10,000 years of climate. On the far right is warming after the Little Ice Age, which would have been the last 150 years or so, with the sudden upturn in warming beginning in 1950. "Unprecedented!" the Alarmists say. "It's the warmest we've ever been."

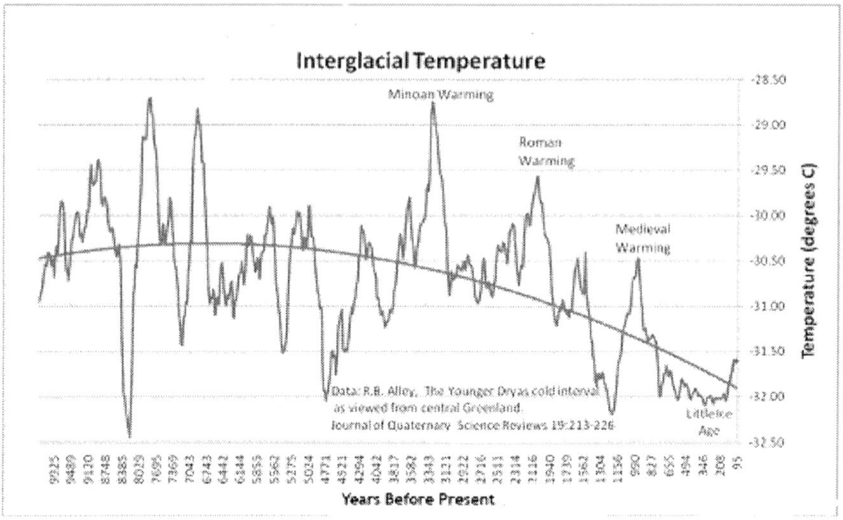

Unprecedented during those 150 years... Maybe. But not even close in the last 4000 years. About 1,000 years ago we had the Medieval Warm Period, where it was significantly warmer. Did humans cause that?

About 2,100 years ago, there was the Roman Warm Period, where it was warmer still. Did humans cause that?

3,300 years ago, the Minoan Warm Period where it was warmer still. Did humans cause that one, too?

The warming of 1978 - 1998 came during one of the coldest periods of the last 10,000 years, and logic would say that it was a natural warming cycle, rebounding from the Little Ice Age.

This next graph definitely scares me more than any other. It's a graph of glacial and interglacial periods that have happened in recent history – roughly every 100,000 years (I spoke of the Milankovitch cycles earlier).

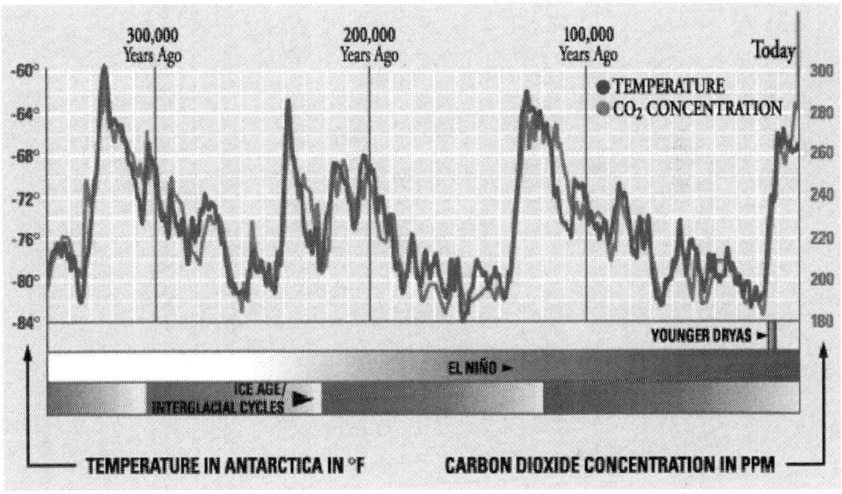

If you start on the lower left, you see a sudden warming to where it peaks and begins to get colder and heads into a glacial period. Then it repeats itself, suddenly warming and then cooling and going into another glacial period. Then the third sudden warming and cooling into a glacial period. And now? Are we headed for the fourth of these repetitive cycles? Maybe facing a turnaround into cooling and another glacial period?

I certainly hope it’s not soon. I would much prefer continued warming.

The next graph doesn't give much encouragement toward my wish for more warming. It's a graph of global temperatures from 1998 – 2014.

If you look at the peak in the year 2000, it's roughly at the same level as 2014. So, other than the usual peaks and valleys, if you drew a horizontal line averaging the temperatures, it would show little or no warming in those 14 years. The next five years, through 2019, would show roughly the same.

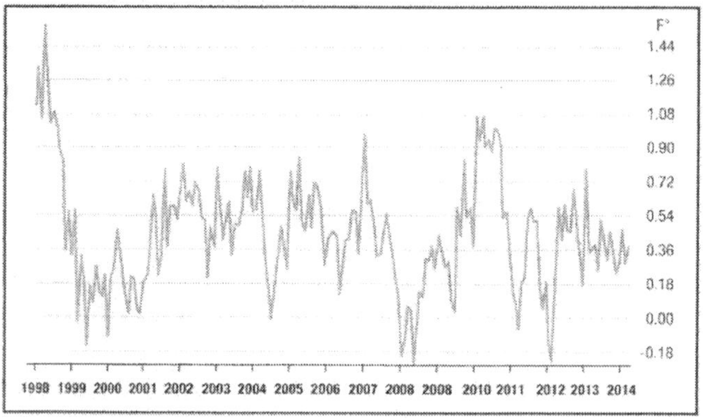

Source: NASA, NOAA and Remote Sensing Systems

Those fighting to hold on to “man-made global warming” (by their fingernails) are announcing "warmest ever" virtually every month of every year lately, while dealing in <u>hundredths of a degree.</u>

I'm afraid they too, may be wishing for continued warming in the not-too-distant future... If Mother Nature decides to turn things the other way.

A Brief Look at Extreme Weather Events.

The disciples of man-made global warming contend that the warming of our climate has:

- Worsened the extreme weather events.

- Bleached coral reefs of their color.

- Worsened wildfires.

- Extremes in precipitation and drought.

A study of historical records shows there is no increase in frequency or intensity of extreme weather events. In fact, frequency and intensity of tornadoes and hurricanes has decreased in the last two decades. However, the IPCC and its disciples, contend that since the planet has been warming, these extreme weather events have increased. Their argument is in terms of "dollars of damage."

While damage from extreme weather events has increased in absolute terms over the last 30 years, once the damage totals are adjusted for increases in population, wealth, higher property values and inflation, the higher cost disappears.

In fact, after adjustments, there has been a downward trend. Since 1990, damages from extreme weather events as a proportion of Global GDP have decreased by nearly 20%.

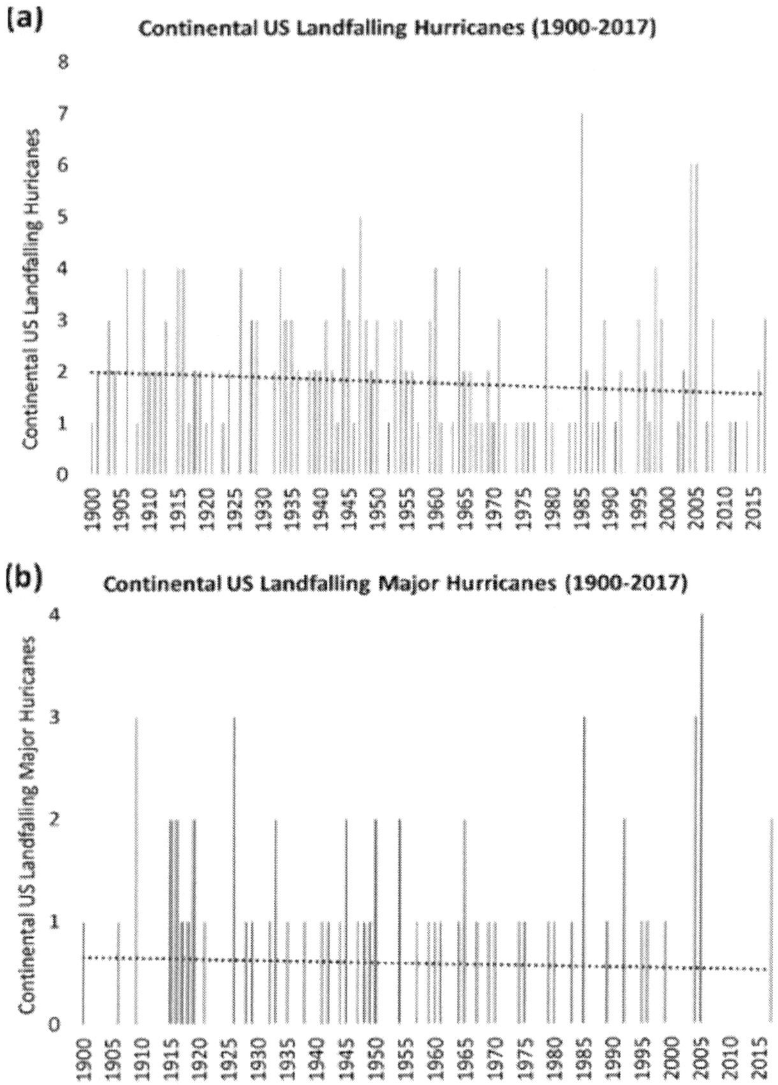

The previous graphs show Hurricane and Major Hurricane landfalls since 1900. The dotted lines show averages, and show slow, steady declines on both charts, including during the recent warming period, 1978-1998.

And, the number of strong and violent tornadoes has decreased over the past 50 years as well.

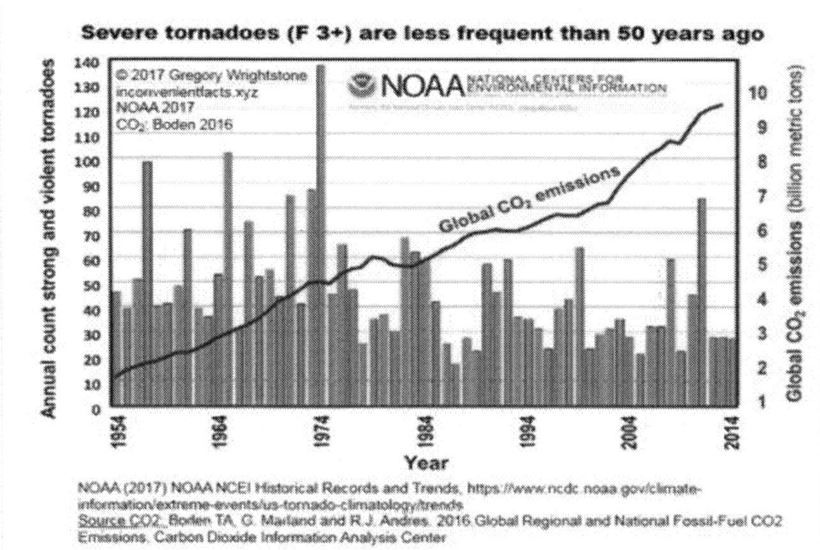

Global Warming has not caused the bleaching of coral reefs. Reefs have come and gone repeatedly for nearly two billion years. Early reefs were bacterial, then, later, multicellular life was the main stay of reefs. Reefs would thrive, supporting multicellular life forms, then they'd come under attack by other organisms, move out and the reef "dies." Eventually, other biological organisms move in, bringing life and color back to the reef.

Other threats to Coral reefs would include large, powerful waves breaking apart the reefs; periods of low tides leaving the coral heads exposed, drying them out and causing them great stress, even death; viruses that can infect reefs and cause death; algae can bloom and negatively affect reefs; excavation, like dredging a canal; over-fishing the reef areas; and many more.

My point is, reefs have come and gone regularly throughout Earth's history, thriving and then dying for many reasons. Now, all of a sudden – in the last few decades – it's Global Warming's fault.

Next was "Wildfires that have worsened because of Global Warming." The following graph shows a steady decline in wildfires decade by decade – likely due to better and better methods of wildfire management.

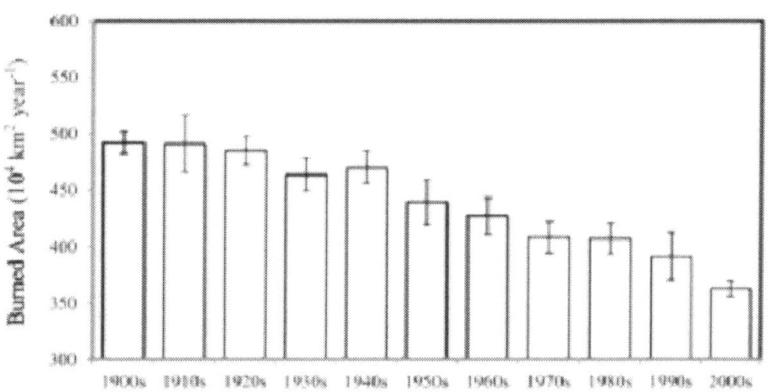

Figure 6. Decadal variation of global burned area. Error bar refers to the standard deviation of annual burned area within that decade.

The final point was the Alarmist's depiction of extremes in precipitation and drought resulting from global warming. The following chart is from the US Bureau of Meteorology and shows no extreme deviation in precipitation over the last century. (It appears there are two or three years missing in the most recent decade.)

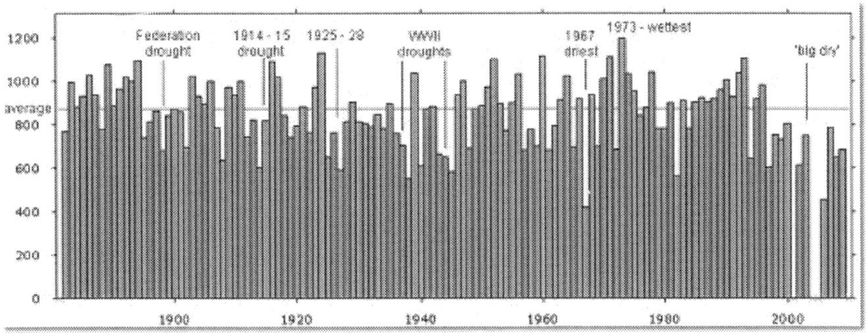

A Brief Look at My Final Thoughts

On the dogma of "Man-Made Global Warming," I am completely baffled that any scientist could support such a fraudulent theory. Except, I suppose, for the huge funding that's available the world over. BUT, what government organization is going to approve funding for a project based on the theory, *"Earth's climate continues to warm and cool in cyclical fashion, as it has for billions of years."*

NONE!

But, develop a theory that contends, *"Earth's climate is warming at a catastrophic rate, all due to emissions of CO2 by human activity, and we must act to stop these emissions immediately or face dire consequences."*

VOILA... Immense funding sources open up to you.

I'm not certain, but I think it was Karl Marx who first said, "Develop a concept and repeat it often enough, it will become the truth and force reality from the argument." The Alarmists have been banging on their "theory" constantly for nearly three decades. Fortunately, they've not been able to completely force reality from the argument... Yet! Hopefully, serious people, scientists and politicians will stand strong against the arrogant, the foolish, the preposterous, the ludicrous....

Patrick Moore, co-founder of Greenpeace contends, "Man-Made Climate Change" is a theory for which there is no scientific proof what-so-ever. There is only a **vigorous, vocal group of activists on the left that are ferociously evangelizing.**

Climate is changing - recently it's been getting warmer - and it has been changing throughout Earth's history. Always has... Always will. We've been through cooling cycles and warming cycles, through Ice Ages, glacial and interglacial periods, all of this for a couple billion years. All of which took place before there was ***any such thing as CO2 emissions from human activity***. Much of it before we Homo Sapiens were walking upright and appreciating this beautiful planet.

Therefore, the ***real causes*** for climate changes (other than "Man-Made") we're at work to bring about the warming and cooling – even the extremes that brought about Ice Ages, then melted away the ice and warmed Earth – long before we were here.

The chart on the next page tracks temperature and CO2 levels for most of Earth's history. Because the original of this chart was in color and easier to differentiate, I'll explain that the temperature track is the upper line on the right two thirds of the chart and the CO2 track is the lower line. No significance to up or down, that's just the way they tracked.

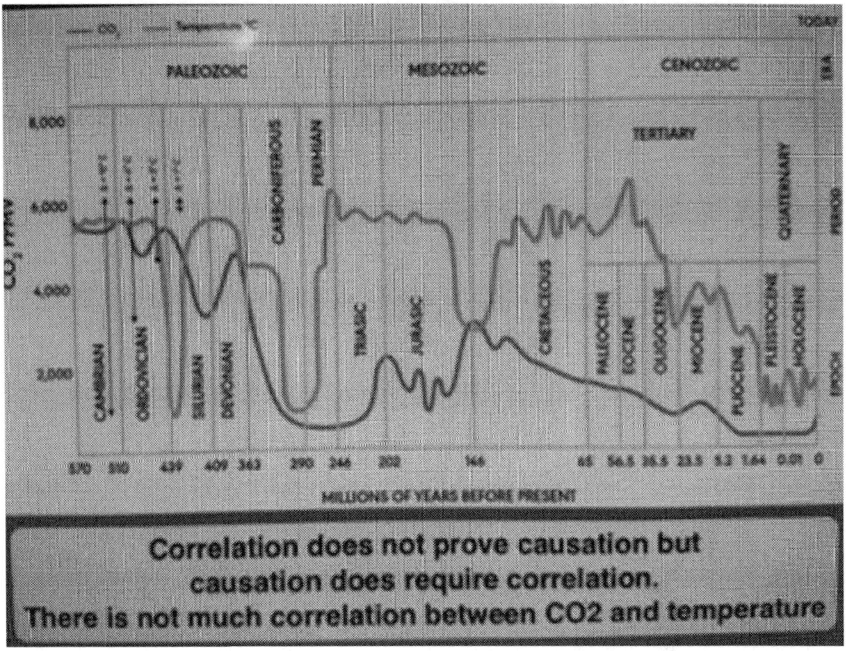

Please, if your eyes glaze over when looking at charts – as mine often do – please give this one a good look. If you follow the warming and cooling cycles (the ups and downs of the top line) it shows you two important things:

1. For the past couple hundred years (lower right), we have been in one of the coolest periods in Earth's history… ever.
2. As it says at the bottom of the chart, there's not a lot of correlation between CO2 levels and temperature. In fact, there are more cycles/trends where temperatures and CO2 levels were going in opposite directions.

The most telling thing about "Man-Made Global Warming" is what they **don't ever** talk about... That we are currently in one of the coolest periods in Earth's history, and slowly climbing out of it... Slowly WARMING.

They love regularly broadcasting alarming news that, "We've set another record for the Warmest month... Warmest year..." whatever. They have ***never*** disclosed to the folks that they hope to alarm with their "sky is falling" news, that they are talking about the ***last 180 years*** (since we began recording weather stats). Stretch this out for the history of planet Earth and we're nowhere near the warmest *anything* as the above chart demonstrates. (Because of "Data Doctoring" – see page 32 – I'm not sure it's even the warmest in the last 180 years.)

Setting that doubt aside, I liken their hue and cry of "Warmest Ever" to being without electricity for two days in January in Minnesota. The temperature in your home has fallen to 39°F and you don't know what you'll do to keep pipes from freezing as it drops more. Finally, thank God, the power company repairs the lines and your electricity comes on. The first thing you hear is the furnace kicking-in. Soon, warm air is flowing and temperature is climbing.

Enter stage left, Al Gore and disciples. They see on your thermostat that the temperature in your home has risen all the way to 62°F and exclaim, "We're immediately shutting down your furnace. Your home is all the way up to 62° and it's the hottest it's ever been!"

Well, if they're referring to the last day and a half, that's true. If they're talking about the history of your home... Not even close.

Fossil fuels have given great things to us – longevity, prosperity, and personal freedoms. AND, a good many of the "Climatista Hippocrates" enjoy the full benefits of fossil fuel with their private jets, high price cars, huge yachts, and large, extravagant homes (as in Al Gore buying a $9 Million mansion on a California beachfront). Meanwhile, they tell the rest of us that we have to stop using fossil fuels.

In the world of economics, corporations of all kinds are told continually by their PR departments and advertising departments to go along with this "warming thing." Studies and focus groups tell them repeatedly, "If we can paint ourselves as more Green than the other guy, then customers will prefer our product over the other guy's."

Meanwhile, worldwide CO2 emissions have grown by 23-29% (depending on your source) since the year 2000. But the temperature these past two decades has pretty much flat-lined. The warming they still insist on proclaiming is in hundredths of a degree – statistically insignificant.

As Ivar Giaever, Norwegian Physicist with a Nobel Prize in Physics, said, "Do they seriously think they can arrive at an average global temperature for all of Earth's differing climates, reach numbers rounded to hundredths, and think that it's meaningful?"

So, CO_2 emissions are up about 26% and no significant warming? Average temperature should have gone up 0.4°C or 0.5°C with that much added CO_2. It's another example highlighting the point that CO_2 does not *cause* warming. Rather, *the myriad of extremely complex systems that influence Earth's climate* worked their magic; put warming on hold while human activities caused emissions of large amounts of CO_2 into the atmosphere.

"Mother Nature" at the helm.

While the Alarmists work to keep our focus on the recent 180 years and that we're reaching "warmer than ever" temperatures, they don't want us to see the big picture that we are, in fact, coming out of one of the coldest periods in a couple billion years. We are in that house that's finally warming up from the cold.

"CO_2 from human activity" was the only contrivance they could come up with that could possibly be controlled, and that most of "the folks" might buy into.

Sorry… I'm not buying.

Made in the USA
Lexington, KY
02 November 2019

56501085R00044